Drilling Machines

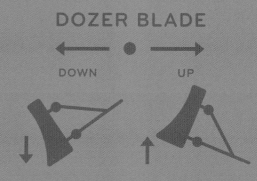

DOZER BLADE

DOWN   UP

Published by Creative Education

P.O. Box 227, Mankato, Minnesota 56002

Creative Education is an imprint of The Creative Company

www.thecreativecompany.us

Design and production by Rob & Damia Design

Art direction by Rita Marshall

Printed in the United States of America

Photographs by Getty Images (Hulton Archive/Getty Images), iStockphoto

(Rob Bouwman, Melissa Carroll, Lya Cattel, Tom Fawls, Michael Fuller,

Joe Gough, Peter Ingvorsen, Iurii Konoval, Steven Robertson, Nicholas Sereno)

Library of Congress Cataloging-in-Publication Data

Gilbert, Sara.

Drilling machines / by Sara Gilbert.

p. cm. — (Machines that build)

Includes index.

ISBN 978-1-58341-729-4

1. Drilling and boring machinery—Juvenile literature. I. Title. II. Series.

TJ1263.G45 2009

621.9'52—dc22   2007051663

First edition

9 8 7 6 5 4 3 2 1

DIESEL FUEL

OFF   ON

ENGINE OIL

SEATBELTS

CREATIVE  EDUCATION

Drilling Machines

sara gilbert
machines that build

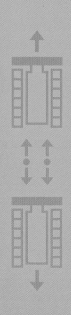

A drilling machine cuts through the ground. Drilling machines work on building sites. They work at mines. They even work in farm fields.

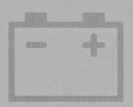

Tall drilling machines can make very deep holes.

5

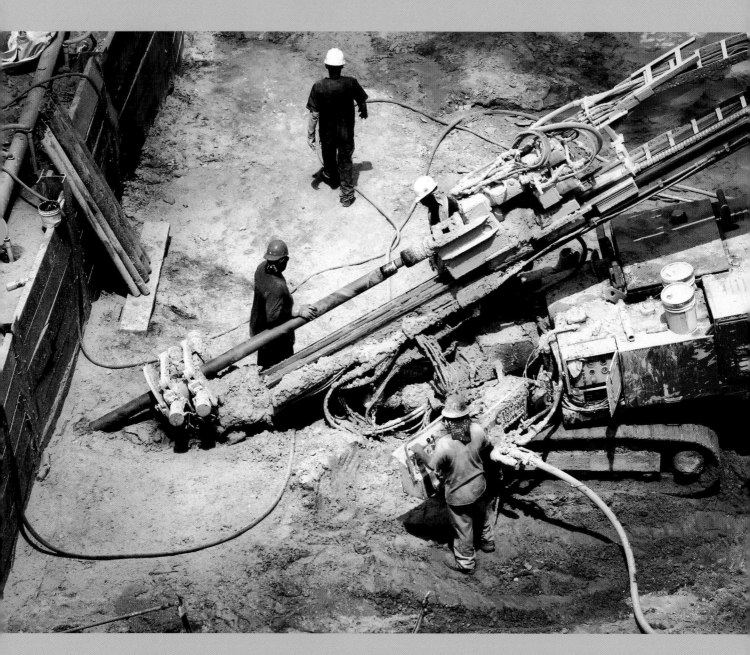

Some machines drill at an angle to the ground.

Drilling machines are used to reach deep into the ground. They find water for wells and *coal* in mines. They help lay underground pipes for water. They help farmers plant seeds.

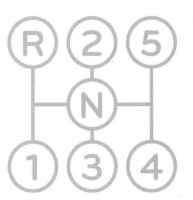

The operator controls
how fast the drill moves.

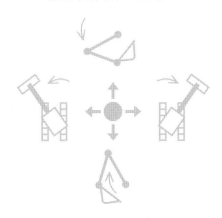

Drilling machines are controlled by an *operator*. The operator sits in a *cab*. The operator can watch the drill go down into the earth. The cab has windows on all sides.

A heavy-duty drill bit

Most drilling machines use tools called drill bits. The bits spin into the ground and make the holes. They are attached to metal pipes called drills. For big jobs, the pipes can be made longer. Then the drill can make a hole that is more than 100 feet (30.5 m) deep!

Very large drills are used at some building sites.

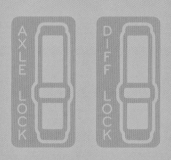

The biggest drilling machines weigh more than 250,000 pounds (113 t). They can hold 800 gallons (3,028 l) of gas, the fuel that makes them go. They move on wide, *steel* belts called crawler tracks. These drilling machines are used in mines.

At some mines, machines drill holes for dynamite.

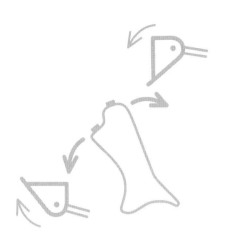

People in *Egypt* used human-powered drilling machines to help build the *pyramids*. In the 1850s, people started using steam-powered drilling machines to drill for water and oil. Today, drilling machines run on fuel like gasoline or electricity.

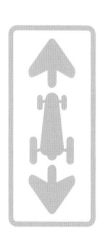

A machine from the early 1900s drills a water well.

*Some drill bits are close
to the drilling machine.*

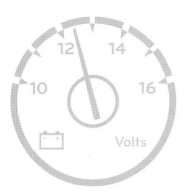

Most drills go straight down into the earth or at a slight angle. Others can drill underneath roads and go around things that might get in the way. They help people put in new pipes without tearing up roads.

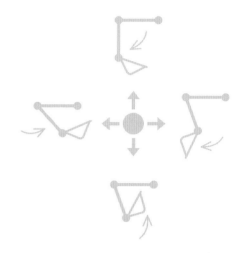

Farmers use seed drills to plant their crops. The seed drills make small holes in the ground. Then seeds are placed in the holes. The drilling machines help farmers plant neat, even rows.

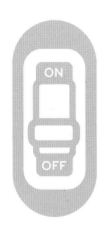

*Small seed drills can attach
to the back of a tractor.*

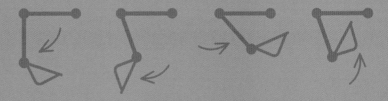

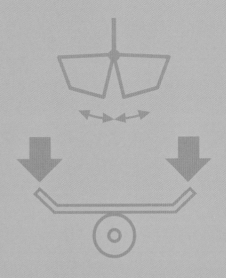

Drilling machines spin through dirt and rocks. When the hole is deep enough, the drill comes back up. Then the drilling machine goes on to its next job!

A heavy-duty drill can blast easily through rocks.

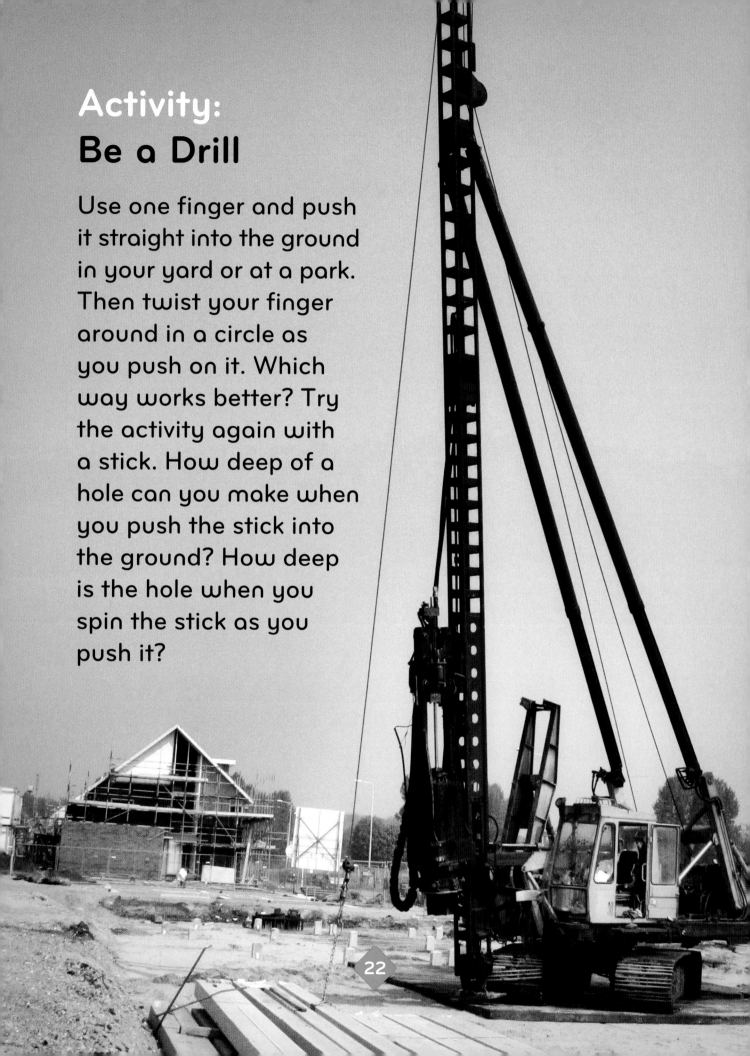

Activity:
Be a Drill

Use one finger and push
it straight into the ground
in your yard or at a park.
Then twist your finger
around in a circle as
you push on it. Which
way works better? Try
the activity again with
a stick. How deep of a
hole can you make when
you push the stick into
the ground? How deep
is the hole when you
spin the stick as you
push it?

Glossary

cab: the place where the operator sits

coal: a black rock found underground that is used for fuel

Egypt: a country in Africa that has a lot of desert

operator: the person who controls a machine

pyramids: huge, triangle-shaped structures built in Egypt; kings were buried in them

steel: a strong material that is hard to break

Read More About It

Llewellyn, Claire. *Mighty Machines: Truck.* New York: DK Publishing, 2000.

Richards, Jon. *Diggers and Other Construction Machines.* Brookfield, Conn.: Millbrook Press, 1999.

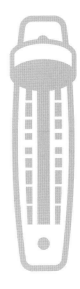

Index

crawler tracks 12

drill bits 11

farms 4, 7, 18

first drilling machines 14

fuel 12, 14

mines 4, 7, 12

operators 9

pyramids 14

roads 17

rocks 21

wells 7